To Christine

A Golden
CHRISTMAS
TREASURY

A Gift for
1989

Your friend always

Love Val.

A Golden
CHRISTMAS TREASURY

COMPILED BY MARK DANIEL

PAVILION
MICHAEL JOSEPH

First published in Great Britain in 1989 by
PAVILION BOOKS LIMITED
196 Shaftesbury Avenue, London WC2H 8JL
in association with Michael Joseph Limited
27 Wrights Lane, Kensington, W8 5TZ

Conceived and produced by Breslich & Foss, London
Anthology copyright © 1989 by Mark Daniel
Design copyright © 1989 by Breslich & Foss

Designed by Roger Daniels

A CIP catalogue record for this book is available from the
British Library

ISBN 1-85145-4632

10 9 8 7 6 5 4 3 2 1

Printed and bound in Italy.

The art for this book consists of full-colour reproductions
of oil paintings from the Edwardian and Victorian eras, as well as
prints of black-and-white engravings from the same periods.
All colour pictures are courtesy of
Fine Art Photographic Library, London.

Contents

CHRISTMAS
IS COMING

The Holly and the Ivy

The Holly and the Ivy
Now they are both full-grown,
Of all the trees that are in the wood,
The Holly bears the crown.

chorus: O, the rising of the sun,
The running of the deer,
The playing of the merry organ,
Sweet singing in the choir.

The Holly bears a blossom
    As white as the lily flower,
And Mary bore sweet Jesus Christ
    To be our sweet Saviour.

The Holly bears a berry,
    As red as any blood,
And Mary bore sweet Jesus Christ
    To do poor sinners good.

The Holly bears a prickle
    As sharp as any thorn,
And Mary bore sweet Jesus Christ
    On Christmas day in the morn.

The Holly bears a bark,
    As bitter as any gall,
And Mary bore sweet Jesus Christ
    For to redeem us all.

The Holly and the Ivy,
    Now they are both full-grown,
Of all the trees that are in the wood,
    The Holly bears the crown.

TRADITIONAL

Deck the Hall

Deck the hall with boughs of holly,
'Tis the season to be jolly,
Don we now our gay apparel,
Troll the ancient yule-tide carol.

See the blazing yule before us,
Strike the harp and join the chorus,
Follow me in merry measure,
While I tell of yule-tide treasure.

Fast away the old year passes,
Hail the new, ye lads and lasses,
Sing we joyous all together,
Heedless of the wind and weather.

WELSH TRADITIONAL CAROL

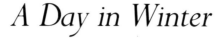

A Day in Winter

Through the Crimson fires of morning
    Streaming upwards in the East,
Leaps the sun, with sudden dawning,
    Like a captive king released;
And December skies reflected
    In the azure hue below
Seem like summer recollected
    In the dreaming of the snow. –
It is winter, little children, let the summer,
             singing, go!

There are crisp winds gaily blowing
    From the North and from the West;
'Bove the river strongly flowing
    Lies the river's frozen breast:
O'er its shining silence crashing
    Skim the skaters to and fro;
And the noonday splendours flashing
    In the rainbow colors show. –
It is winter, little children, let the summer,
             singing, go!

When the gorgeous day is dying,
    There is swept a cloud of rose
O'er the hill-tops softly lying
    In the flush of sweet repose;
And the nests, all white with snowing,
    In the twilight breezes blow;
And the untired moon is showing
    Her bare heart to the snow. –
It is winter, little children, let the summer,
             singing, go!

MRS L. C. WHITON
Christmas Carols and Midsummer Songs, 1881

And I *do* come home at Christmas. We all do, or we all should. We all come home, or ought to come home, for a short holiday – the longer, the better – from the great boarding school, where we are for ever working at our arithmetical slates, to take, and give a rest.

CHARLES DICKENS
Dr Marigold's Prescription

A Jewel Day

O Children, wake, for a fairy world
    Is waiting for you and me,
With gems aglow on the meadow grass,
    And jewels on every tree.

The hedgerows glitter, the dark woods shine
    In dresses of sparkling white,
For while we slumbered, the Ice Queen passed
    All over the earth last night.

LUCY DIAMOND

Robin Redbreast

Good-bye, good-bye to summer!
For summer's nearly done;
The garden's smiling faintly,
Cool breezes in the sun;
Our thrushes now are silent,
Our swallows flown away –
But Robin's here, in coat of brown,
With ruddy breast-knot gay.
Robin, Robin Redbreast,
O Robin dear!
Robin singing sweetly
In the falling of the year.

Bright yellow, red, and orange,
The leaves come down in hosts;
The trees are Indian princes,
But soon they'll turn to ghosts;
The leathery pears and apples
Hang russet on the bough,
It's autumn, autumn, autumn late,
'Twill soon be winter now.
Robin, Robin Redbreast,
O Robin dear!
And what will this poor Robin do?
For pinching days are near.

The fireside for the cricket,
The wheatstack for the mouse,
When trembling night-winds whistle
And moan all round the house;
The frosty ways like iron,
The branches plumed with snow –
Alas! in winter, dead and dark,
Where can poor Robin go?
Robin, Robin Redbreast,
O Robin dear!
And a crumb of bread for Robin
His little heart to cheer.

WILLIAM ALLINGHAM

Winter

A wrinkled, crabbed man they picture thee,
   Old Winter, with a rugged beard as grey
As the long moss upon the apple-tree;
Blue lipt, an ice-drop at thy sharp blue nose;
   Close muffled up, and on thy dreary way,
Plodding alone through sleet and drifting snows.

They should have drawn thee by the high-heapt hearth,
   Old Winter! seated in thy great armed chair,
Watching the children at their Christmas mirth,
   Or circled by them, as thy lips declare
Some merry jest, or tale of murder dire,
   Or troubled spirit that disturbs the night,
Pausing at times to rouse the mouldering fire,
   Or taste the old October brown and bright.

ROBERT SOUTHEY

Christmas Is Coming

Christmas is coming,
   The Goose is getting fat,
Please put a penny in the old man's hat.
   If you haven't a penny, a ha' penny will do,
   If you haven't a ha' penny – God bless you!

TRADITIONAL CHILDREN'S RHYME

The Whisper-Whisper Man

The Whisper-Whisper man
Makes all the wind in the world.
He has a gown as brown as brown;
His hair is long and curled.

In the stormy winter-time
He taps at your window-pane,
And all the night, until it's light,
He whispers through the rain.

If you peeped through a Fairy-Ring
You'd see him, little and brown;
You'd hear the beat of his clackety feet
Scampering through the town.

THORA STOWELL

The North Wind

The north wind doth blow,
And we shall have snow,
And what will poor robin do then, poor thing?
O, he'll go to the barn,
And to keep himself warm
He'll hide his head under his wing, poor thing.

The north wind doth blow,
And we shall have snow,
And what will the swallow do then, poor thing?
O, do you not know,
He's gone long ago
To a country much warmer than ours, poor thing?

The north wind doth blow,
And we shall have snow,
And what will the dormouse do then, poor thing?
Rolled up in a ball,
In his nest snug and small,
He'll sleep till the winter is past, poor thing?

The north wind doth blow,
And we shall have snow,
And what will the children do then, poor things?
O, when lessons are done,
They'll jump, skip, and run,
And play till they make themselves warm, poor things.

ANON

CHRISTMAS
EVE

Silent Night

Silent night, holy night,
All is calm, all is bright
Round yon Virgin mother and child
  Holy infant so tender and mild,
Sleep in heavenly peace,
  Sleep in heavenly peace.

Silent night, holy night,
  Shepherds quake at the sight;
Glories stream from heaven afar,
  Heavenly hosts sing Alleluia,
Christ the Saviour is born,
  Christ the Saviour is born.

Silent night, holy night,
  Son of God, love's pure light
Radiant beams from thy holy face,
  With the dawn of redeeming grace,
Jesus, Lord, at thy birth,
  Jesus, Lord, at thy birth.

Silent Night was written on Christmas Eve, 1818, in Oberndorf, Austria, near Salzburg. A hungry mouse had eaten through the leather of the organ bellows, so Joseph Mohr, the priest, and Franz Gruber, the organist, had to compose a carol for children's voices and guitar at short notice. The fame of *Silent Night* spread slowly and by a series of coincidences throughout the world, but it was not until 1867 that the song was published under the names of its true composers. By then, both men were dead.

The Snow Lies White on Roof and Tree

The snow lies white on roof and tree,
  Frost fairies creep about,
The world's as still as it can be,
  And Santa Claus is out.

He's making haste his gifts to leave,
  While the stars show his way,
There'll soon be no more Christmas Eve,
  Tomorrow's Christmas Day!

ANON

And there were in the same country shepherds abiding in the field, keeping watch over their flock by night.

And lo, the angel of the Lord came upon them, and the glory of the Lord shone about them: and they were sore afraid.

And the angel said unto them, "Fear not: for, behold, I bring you good tidings of great joy, which shall be to all people.

"For unto you is born this day in the city of David a Saviour, which is Christ the Lord.

"And this shall be a sign unto you: Ye shall find the babe wrapped in swaddling clothes, lying in a manger."

And suddenly there was with the angel a multitude of the heavenly host praising God, and saying,

"Glory to God in the highest, and on earth peace, goodwill toward men."

ST LUKE'S GOSPEL
2.8-14

The Legend of the Christmas Rose

Legend says that a little shepherd girl of Bethlehem followed after the shepherds who had received the angels' message and were journeying to the stable. All the shepherds took along gifts for the Christ child; but the little girl had no gift to give. As she lagged behind the others, somewhat sad at heart, there suddenly appeared an angel in a glow of light, who scattered beautiful white roses in her path. Eagerly she gathered them in her arms and laid them at the manger as her gift to the little Lord Jesus.

The Oxen

Christmas Eve, and twelve of the clock.
    "Now they are all on their knees,"
An elder said as we sat in a flock
    By the embers in hearthside ease.

We pictured the meek mild creatures where
    They dwelt in their strawy pen,
Nor did it occur to one of us there
    To doubt they were kneeling then.

So fair a fancy few would weave
    In these years! Yet, I feel
If someone said on Christmas Eve,
    "Come, see the oxen kneel

"In the lonely barton by yonder coomb
    Our childhood used to know,"
I should go with him in the gloom,
    Hoping it might be so.

THOMAS HARDY

As Joseph Was
A-Walking

As Joseph was a-walking,
   He heard an angel sing:
"This night shall be born
   Our heavenly King.

"He neither shall be born
   In housen or in hall,
Nor in the place of Paradise,
   But in an ox's stall.

"He neither shall be clothed
   In purple nor in pall,
But all in fair linen
   As wear babies all.

"He neither shall be rocked
   In silver nor in gold
But in a wooden cradle
   That rocks upon the mould.

"He neither shall be christened
   In white wine or in red,
But with fair spring water
   With which we were christened."

ANON
The Cherry Tree Carol

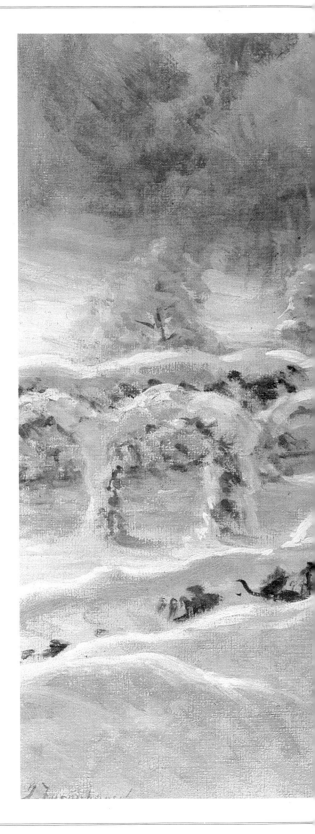

Winter Time

Late lies the wintry sun abed,
   A frosty, fiery sleepy-head;
Blinks but an hour or two; and then,
   A blood red orange, sets again.

Before the stars have left the skies,
   At morning in the dark I rise;
And shivering in my nakedness,
   By the cold candle, bathe and dress.

Close by the jolly fire I sit
   To warm my frozen bones a bit;
Or with a reindeer-sled, explore
   The colder countries round the door.

When to go out, my nurse doth wrap
   Me in my comforter and cap,
The cold wind burns my face, and blows
   Its frosty pepper up my nose.

Black are my steps on silver sod;
   Thick blows my frosty breath abroad;
And tree and house, and hill and lake,
   Are frosted like a wedding-cake.

ROBERT LOUIS STEVENSON

Infant Holy, Infant Lowly

Infant holy, infant lowly,
For his bed a cattle stall;
Oxen lowing, little knowing,
Christ the babe is Lord of all.
Swift are winging angels singing,
Noels ringing, tidings bringing,
Christ the babe is Lord of all,
Christ the babe is Lord of all.

Flocks were sleeping, shepherds keeping,
Vigil till the morning new,
Saw the glory, heard the story,
Tidings of a gospel true.
Thus rejoicing, free from sorrow,
Praises voicing greet the morrow,
Christ the babe was born for you,
Christ the babe was born for you.

POLISH CAROL

Away in a Manger

Away in a manger,
    No crib for a bed,
The little Lord Jesus
    Laid down his sweet head.
The stars in the bright sky
    Look'd down where he lay,
The little Lord Jesus
    Asleep on the hay.

The cattle are lowing,
    The baby awakes,
But little Lord Jesus,
    No crying he makes.
I love thee Lord Jesus,
    Look down from the sky,
And stay by my cradle
    Till morning is nigh.

Be near me Lord Jesus;
    I ask thee to stay
Close by me forever
    And love me, I pray.
Bless all the dear children
    In thy tender care,
And fit us for heaven
    To live with thee there.

ANON

How the Fir-Tree Became the Christmas Tree

The fir is a humble tree, yet it is by merit of that very humility that it became honored and adorned in our homes at Christmas.

When Christ was born, all creation was happy. Birds, beasts, trees, and flowers drew near to declare allegiance and to bring him gifts. "I," said the palm tree which stood by the stable, "I shall give him my finest leaf to fan him in the summer."

"And I," said the olive, "I shall give him my sweetest oil with which he shall anoint himself."

"And I," said the fir-tree, "what can I give him?"

"Nothing," snapped the others in chorus. "Your tears are sticky and your needles would prick his soft skin."

"Yes," the fir-tree sadly nodded his head, "you are right. I have nothing worthy to be given to the Christ-child."

But an angel standing nearby had heard this exchange and felt sorry for the modest fir-tree. When darkness fell, therefore, he asked a few of the smaller stars to come and sit on the fir-tree's branches. At that moment baby Jesus opened his eyes and the sight of the sparkling tree made him smile with delight.

As the years went by and more and more people celebrated his birthday, Jesus asked Father Christmas to place a fir-tree adorned with candles in every home so that other children could see what he once saw. Thus was the fir-tree's meekness rewarded, for no other tree shines on so many happy faces.

O Little Town
of Bethlehem

O little town of Bethlehem,
How still we see thee lie!
Above thy deep and dreamless sleep
The silent stars go by.
Yet in thy dark streets shineth
The everlasting light;
The hopes and fears of all the years
Are met in thee tonight.

O morning stars, together
    Proclaim the holy birth,
And praises sing to God the King,
    And peace to men on earth.
For Christ is born of Mary
    And gather'd all above,
While mortals sleep, the angels keep
    Their watch of wond'ring love.

How silently, how silently,
    The wondrous gift is giv'n!
So God imparts to human hearts
    The blessings of his heav'n.
No ear may hear his coming;
    But in this world of sin,
Where meek souls will receive him, still
    The dear Christ enters in.

O holy child of Bethlehem,
    Descend to us, we pray;
Cast out our sin and enter in,
    Be born in us today.
We hear the Christmas angels
    The great glad tidings tell:
O come to us, abide with us,
    Our Lord Emmanuel.

PHILLIPS BROOKS

How Far Is It to Bethlehem?

How far is it to Bethlehem?
  Not very far.
Shall we find the stable-room
  Lit by a star?

Can we see the little Child,
  Is he within?
If we lift the wooden latch
  May we go in?

May we stroke the creatures there,
  Ox, ass, or sheep?
May we peep like them and see
  Jesus asleep?

If we touch his tiny hand
  Will he awake?
Will he know we've come so far
  Just for his sake?

Great kings have precious gifts,
  And we have nought,
Little smiles and little tears
  Are all we brought.

For all weary children
  Mary must weep.
Here, on his bed of straw
  Sleep, children, sleep.

God in his mother's arms,
  Babes in the byre,
Sleep, as they sleep who find
  Their heart's desire.

FRANCES CHESTERTON

Sly Santa Claus

All the house was asleep,
    And the fire burning low,
When, from far up the chimney,
    Came down a "Ho! ho!"
And a little, round man,
    With a terrible scratching,
Dropped into the room
    With a wink that was catching.
Yes, down he came, bumping,
And thumping, and jumping,
    And picking himself up without sign
        of a bruise!

"Ho! ho!" he kept on,
　　As if bursting with cheer.
"Good children, gay children,
　　Glad children, see here!
I have brought you fine dolls,
　　And gay trumpets, and rings,
Noah's arks, and bright skates,
　　And a host of good things!
I have brought a whole sackful,
A packful, a hackful!
Come hither, come hither, come hither
　　　and choose!

"Ho! ho! What is this?
　　Why, they all are asleep!
But their stockings are up,
　　And my presents will keep!
So, in with the candies,
　　The books, and the toys;
All the goodies I have
　　For the good girls and boys.
I'll ram them, and jam them,
And slam them, and cram them;
　　All the stockings will hold while the
　　　tired youngsters snooze."

All the while his round shoulders
　　Kept ducking and ducking;
And his little, fat fingers
　　Kept tucking and tucking;
Until every stocking
　　Bulged out, on the wall,
As if it were bursting,
　　And ready to fall.
And then, all at once,
　　With a whisk and a whistle,
And twisting himself
　　Like a tough bit of gristle,
He bounced up again,
　　Like the down of a thistle.
　　And nothing was left but the prints
　　　of his shoes.

MRS C. S. STONE

A Visit from St. Nicholas

Twas the night before Christmas, when all through the house
Not a creature was stirring, not even a mouse;
The stockings were hung by the chimney with care,
In hopes that St. Nicholas soon would be there;
The children were nestled all snug in their beds,
While visions of sugar-plums danced in their heads;
And mamma in her 'kerchief, and I in my cap,
Had just settled our brains for a long winter's nap –
When out on the lawn there arose such a clatter,
I sprang from my bed to see what was the matter.
Away to the window I flew like a flash,
Tore open the shutters, and threw up the sash.
The moon, on the breast of the new-fallen snow,
Gave the luster of midday to objects below;
When, what to my wondering eyes should appear,
But a miniature sleigh and eight tiny reindeer,
With a little old driver, so lively and quick,
I knew in a moment it must be St. Nick.
More rapid than eagles his coursers they came,
And he whistled, and shouted, and called them by name:
"Now, *Dasher!* now, *Dancer!* now, *Prancer* and *Vixen!*
On, *Comet!* on, *Cupid!* on, *Donner* and *Blitzen!*"
To the top of the porch! to the top of the wall!
Now dash away! dash away! dash away all!"
As dry leaves that before the wild hurricane fly,
When they meet with an obstacle, mount to the sky;
So up to the house-top the coursers they flew
With the sleigh full of toys, and St. Nicholas too.

And then, in a twinkling, I heard on the roof
    The prancing and pawing of each little hoof –
As I drew in my head, and was turning around,
    Down the chimney St. Nicholas came with a bound.
He was dressed all in fur, from his head to his foot,
    And his clothes were all tarnished with ashes and soot;
A bundle of toys he had flung on his back,
    And he looked like a pedlar just opening his pack.
His eyes – how they twinkled; his dimples, how merry!
    His cheeks were like roses, his nose like a cherry!
His droll little mouth was drawn up like a bow,
    And the beard of his chin was as white as the snow;
The stump of a pipe he held tight in his teeth,
    And the smoke it encircled his head like a wreath;
He had a broad face and a little round belly
    That shook, when he laughed, like a bowl full of jelly.
He was chubby and plump, a right jolly old elf,
    And I laughed when I saw him, in spite of myself;
A wink of his eye and a twist of his head
    Soon gave me to know I had nothing to dread;
He spoke not a word, but went straight to his work,
    And filled all the stockings; then turned with a jerk,
And laying his finger aside of his nose,
    And giving a nod, up the chimney he rose;
He sprang to his sleigh, to his team gave a whistle,
    And away they all flew like the down of a thistle.
But I heard him exclaim, ere he drove out of sight,
    "Happy Christmas to all, and to all a good night!"

CLEMENT CLARKE MOORE
Troy Sentinel, 23 December 1823

Not believe in Santa Claus! You might as well not
believe in fairies ....Nobody sees Santa Claus, but
this is no sign there is no Santa Claus. The most real things
in the world are these which neither children nor men can see.
No Santa Claus! Thank God! he lives and he lives forever.

FRANK CHURCH
Is There a Santa Claus?, 1897

The Yule Log

Part must be kept wherewith to tend
The Christmas log next year;
And where 'tis safely kept, the fiend
Can do no mischief there.

TRADITIONAL

The yule log is a long-established village tradition. A great tree is selected the previous Candlemas (February 2nd), chopped down, set on fire and left to burn until sundown. This merely serves to blacken the bark. The log is then left until the following Christmas Eve when, with much shouting, singing and dancing, it is dragged by the villagers to the great hall. It is welcomed with even more celebration, garlanded with ribbons and raised on stones at the center of the hall. Brands are placed beneath it and lit with a portion of the previous year's log. The splinter of last year's log is also said to protect the house from fire.

Ceremony for Christmas Eve

Come bring with a noise,
My merry merry boys
The Christmas log to the firing;
While my good dame, she
Bids ye all be free,
And drink to your hearts desiring.
With the last year's brand
Light the new block, and
For good success in his spending,
On your psaltries play
That sweet luck may
Come while the log is a tending.
Drink now the strong beer,
Cut the white loaf here,
The while the meat is a shredding,
For the rare mince-pie;
And the plums stand by
To fill the paste that's a kneading.

ROBERT HERRICK

In the Bleak
Mid-Winter

In the bleak mid-winter
  Frosty wind made moan,
Earth stood hard as iron,
Water like a stone;
Snow had fallen, snow on snow,
Snow on snow,
In the bleak mid-winter,
Long ago.

Our God, heav'n cannot hold him
Nor earth sustain;
Heav'n and earth shall flee away
When he comes to reign:
In the bleak mid-winter
A stable place sufficed
The Lord God Almighty
Jesus Christ.

Enough for him, whom cherubim
Worship night and day,
A breastful of milk
And a mangerful of hay;
Enough for him, whom angels
Fall down before,
The ox and ass and camel
Which adore.

Angels and Archangels
May have gathered there,
Cherubim and Seraphim
Throngèd the air:
But only his mother
In her maiden bliss
Worshipped the beloved
With a kiss.

What can I give him,
Poor as I am?
If I were a shepherd
I would bring a lamb;
If I were a wise man
I would do my part;
Yet what I can I give him –
Give my heart.

CHRISTINA ROSSETTI
Sing-Song, 1872

The Wassail Song

Here we come a-wassailing
　　Among the leaves so green,
Here we come a-wandering,
　　So fair to be seen.

CHORUS: Love and joy come to you,
*　　And to you your wassail too,*
And God bless you, and send you
*　　A happy new year.*

We are not daily beggars
　　That beg from door to door,
But we are neighbors' children
　　Whom you have seen before.

Good Master and good Mistress,
　　As you sit by the fire,
Pray think of us poor children
　　Who are wandering in the mire.

We have a little purse
　　Made of ratching leather skin;
We want some of your small change
　　To line it well within.

Call up the butler of this house,
　　Put on his golden ring;
Let him bring us a glass of beer,
　　And the better we shall sing.

Bring us out a table,
    And spread it with a cloth;
Bring us out a mouldy cheese
    And some of your Christmas loaf.

God bless the Master of this house,
    Likewise the Mistress too,
And all the little children
    That round the table go.

TRADITIONAL
Christmas Anthology, 1906

WASSAILING

Modern bands of carol-singers who go from house to
house are the descendants of the old 'wassailers' who
also went singing all about the town on Christmas Eve. They
presented householders with sprigs of mistletoe or holly and
were welcomed in to drink their hosts' health from the
wassail-bowl. The wassail-bowl was filled with warming
'lamb's wool,' strong beer with nutmeg, sugar, and hot
roasted apples.

MERRY
CHRISTMAS

The fire was blazing brightly under the influence of the bellows, and the kettle was singing gaily under the influence of both. A small tray of tea-things was arranged on the table, a plate of hot buttered toast was gently simmering before the fire, and the red-nosed man himself was busily engaged in converting a large slice of bread into the same agreeable edible, through the instrumentality of a long brass toasting-fork.

CHARLES DICKENS
Pickwick Papers

CINNAMON TOAST

1 tablespoon ground cinnamon
2 tablespoons caster sugar
several slices hot buttered toast

Mix the spice and sugar together. Sprinkle
the mixture on the hot buttered toast.

Christmas Daybreak

Before the paling of the stars,
    Before the winter morn,
Before the earliest cockcrow,
    Jesus Christ was born:
Born in a stable,
    Cradled in a manger,
In the world His hands had made,
    Born a stranger.

Priest and king lay fast asleep
    In Jerusalem,
Young and old lay fast asleep
    In crowded Bethlehem:
Saint and angel, ox and ass,
    Kept a watch together,
Before the Christmas daybreak
    In the winter weather.

Jesus on His Mother's breast
    In the stable cold,
Spotless Lamb of God was He,
    Shepherd of the fold.
Let us kneel with Mary Maid,
    With Joseph bent and hoary,
With saint and angel, ox and ass,
    To hail the King of Glory.

CHRISTINA ROSSETTI

Skating

And in the frosty season, when the sun
Was set, and visible for many a mile
The cottage windows blazed through twilight gloom,
I heeded not their summons: happy time
It was indeed for all of us – for me
It was a time of rapture! Clear and loud
The village clock tolled six, – I wheeled about
Proud and exulting like an untired horse
That cares not for his home. All shod with steel,
We hissed along the polished ice in games
Confederate, imitative of the chase
And woodland pleasures, – the resounding horn,
The pack loud chiming, and the hunted hare.

WILLIAM WORDSWORTH

N ow Christmas is come
    Let us beat up the drum
And call all our neighbors together;
    And when they appear,
Let us make such good cheer
    As will keep out the wind and the weather!

TRADITIONAL

M any merry Christmases, friendships, great
    accumulation of cheerful recollections, affection
on earth, and Heaven at last for all of us.

CHARLES DICKENS
A Christmas wish to his friend John Forster, 1846

The Sunny Bank

As I sat on a sunny bank,
    A sunny bank, a sunny bank,
As I sat on a sunny bank
    On Christmas day in the morning.

I spy'd three ships come sailing by,
    Come sailing by, come sailing by,
I spy'd three ships come sailing by
    On Christmas day in the morning.

And who should be with these three ships,
    With these three ships, with these three ships,
And who should be with these three ships,
    But Joseph and his fair lady.

O he did whistle and she did sing,
    And all the bells on earth did ring
For joy that our Saviour he was born
    On Christmas day in the morning.

TRADITIONAL
A Good Christmas Box, 1847

Now Thrice Welcome, Christmas

Now thrice welcome, Christmas,
  Which brings us good cheer,
Minced pies and plum porridge,
  Good ale and strong beer;
With pig, goose, and capon,
  The best that may be,
So well doth the weather
  And our stomachs agree.

ANON

Peace on Earth, Goodwill to Men...

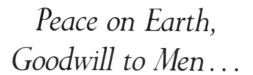

When as you sing of Christmas cheer
   And welcome in the bright new year,
And feast and laugh and dance and play
   And open gifts on Christmas Day,
Pause as you hear the angels' words,
   And don't neglect the little birds.

ANON
Christmas Roses, 1909

The First Noel

T he first Noel the angel did say,
    Was to certain poor shepherds in fields as they lay;
In fields where they lay keeping their sheep,
    On a cold winter's night that was so deep.

CHORUS: Noel, Noel, Noel, Noel,
Born is the King of Israel.

They looked up and saw a Star,
    Shining in the East, beyond them far,
And to the earth it gave great light,
    And so it continued both day and night.

And by the light of that same Star,
    Three Wisemen came from country far;
To seek for a King was their intent,
    And to follow the Star wherever it went.

This Star drew nigh to the north-west,
    O'er Bethlehem it took its rest,
And there it did both stop and stay,
    Right over the place where Jesus lay.

Then entered in those Wisemen three,
    Full reverently upon their knee,
And offered there, in His Presence,
    Their gold, and myrrh, and frankincense.

Then let us all with one accord,
    Sing praises to our heavenly Lord,
That hath made heaven and earth of nought,
    And with His Blood mankind hath bought.

TRADITIONAL
Christmas Anthology, 1906

The Holly Bough

The Cheerful days of Spring are fine,
When sunshine decks the hours,
And blithesome summer, when we twine
Wreaths of the fairest flowers;
But oh! tho' bright the days of Spring,
And Summer's flowrets gay,
There's none that half the pleasure brings
Of merry Christmas Day!

'Tis then from house to house we roam
To sing, as we do now,
And on the mantlepiece at home
We place the holly bough;
And fires ne'er seem to burn so bright,
Nor hearts to be so gay,
Nor feet to tread the ground so light,
As on a Christmas Day!

But cold and selfish should we be,
And heartless, did we fail
To wish that you as well as we,
May merry be and hale!
May he whose love has ever blest
The righteous with its ray,
Grant you all good – and 'midst the rest
A merry Christmas Day!

ANON

The Twelve Days
of Christmas

On the first day of Christmas
my true love sent to me
a partridge in a pear tree.

On the second day of Christmas
my true love sent to me
two turtle doves and a partridge etc.

On the third day of Christmas
my true love sent to me
three French hens, two turtle doves etc.

On the fourth day of Christmas
my true love sent to me
four calling birds, three French hens etc.

On the fifth day of Christmas
my true love sent to me
five gold rings, four calling birds etc.

On the sixth day of Christmas
my true love sent to me
six geese a-laying, five gold rings etc.

On the seventh day of Christmas
my true love sent to me
seven swans a-swimming, six geese a-laying etc.

On the eighth day of Christmas
my true love sent to me
eight maids a-milking, seven swans a-swimming etc.

On the ninth day of Christmas
my true love sent to me
nine ladies dancing, eight maids a-milking etc.

On the tenth day of Christmas
my true love sent to me
ten lords a-leaping, nine ladies dancing etc.

On the eleventh day of Christmas
my true love sent to me
eleven pipers piping, ten lords a-leaping etc.

On the twelfth day of Christmas
my true love sent to me
twelve drummers drumming, eleven pipers piping etc.

TRADITIONAL

CHRISTMAS CHEER

We Wish You a Merry Christmas

We wish you a merry Christmas,
We wish you a merry Christmas,
We wish you a merry Christmas
And a happy New Year.

REFRAIN: Good tidings we bring to you and your kin;
We wish you a merry Christmas and a happy New Year.

Now bring us some figgy pudding,
Now bring us some figgy pudding,
Now bring us some figgy pudding,
And bring some out here.

For we all like figgy pudding,
We all like figgy pudding,
We all like figgy pudding,
So bring some out here.

And we won't go till we've got some,
We won't go till we've got some,
We won't go till we've got some,
So bring some out here.

TRADITIONAL ENGLISH CAROL

Brawn, Pudding, and Souse

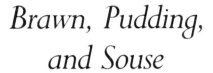

Brawn, pudding, and souse,
  and good mustard withal,
Beef, mutton, and pork shred
   pies of the best,
Pig, veal, goose, and capon
   and turkey well dressed,
Cheese, apples, and nuts, jolly carols to hear,
As them in the country is counted good cheer.

THOMAS TUSSER
(1524-80)

Riddles

L ittle Nancy Etticoat
  In a white petticoat,
And a red rose.
The longer she stands
The shorter she grows.

[A candle]

In marble walls as white as milk,
  Lined with a skin as soft as silk;
Within a fountain crystal clear,
A golden apple doth appear.
No doors there are to this stronghold,
Yet things break in and steal the gold.

[An egg]

I went to the wood and got it;
  I sat me down and looked at it;
The more I looked at it the less I liked it;
And I brought it home because I couldn't help it.

[A thorn]

Old mother Twitchett had but one eye,
  And a long tail which she let fly;
And every time she went over a gap,
She left a bit of her tail in a trap.

[A needle and thread]

I have a little sister, they call her Peep, Peep;
  She wades the waters deep, deep, deep;
She climbs the mountains high, high, high;
Poor little creature she has but one eye.

[A star]

Flour of England, fruit of Spain,
  Met together in a shower of rain;
Put in a bag tied round with a string,
If you'll tell me this riddle, I'll give you a ring.

[A plum pudding]

God Bless the Master

God bless the master of this house,
The mistress bless also,
And all the little children
That round the table go;

And all your kin and kinsmen,
That dwell both far and near;
I wish you a Merry Christmas,
And a happy New Year.

ANON

Hey! Hey! Hey! Hey!
   The boar's head is armèd gay.

The boar's head in hand I bring
With garlands gay encircling,
I pray you all with me to sing
    With Hey!

Lords, knights, and squires,
Parsons, priests, and vicars,
The boar's head is the first mess
    With Hey!

The boar's head, as I now say,
Takes its leave and goes away,
Goeth after the Twelfth Day
    With Hey!

Then comes in the second course with great pride,
The cranes, the herons, the bitterns, by their side,
The partridges, the plovers, the woodcocks, and the snipe,
Larks in hot show, for the ladies to pick,
Good drink also, luscious and fine,
Blood of Allemaine, romany and wine,
    With Hey!

Good brewed ale and wine, I dare well say,
The boar's head with mustard armèd so gay,
Fumity for pottage, and venison fine,
And the humbles of the doe and all that ever comes in,
Capons well baked, with knuckles of the roe,
Raisins and currants and other spices too,
    With Hey!

ANON
15th Century ms. From Reliquiae Antiquae.

THE BOAR'S HEAD

Once considered a rare delicacy, the Boar's head was the traditional first course of the great Christmas feast. Even so, it seems that it was more a symbol than an actual source of food; no matter how large the feast, guests were usually served only one of these treats.

The tradition of the boar's head comes originally from Scandinavian legend: In Valhalla, the Norse warriors' heaven, every day was spent in combat. But come nightfall all fighters' wounds would be healed, and they would feast on the great boar, Soehrimmer. Fortunately he, too, was made whole each day!

Mother Eve's Pudding

If you want a good pudding, to teach you I'm willing;
   Take four pennyworth of eggs, when six for a shilling;
And of the same fruit that Eve had once chosen,
   Well pared and well chopped, at least half a dozen;
Six ounces of bread (let your maid eat the crust),
   The crumbs must be grated as small as the dust;
Six ounces of currants from the stones you must sort,
   Lest they break your teeth, and spoil all your sport;
Six ounces of sugar won't make it too sweet;
   Some salt and some nutmeg will make it complete;
Three hours let it boil, without hurry or flutter,
   And then serve it up, without sugar or butter.

ANON

There never was such a goose. Bob said he didn't believe there ever was such a goose cooked. Its tenderness and flavour, size and cheapness, were the themes of universal admiration. Eked out by apple-sauce and mashed potatoes, it was a sufficient dinner for the whole family; indeed, as Mrs Cratchit said with great delight (surveying one small atom of a bone upon the dish), they hadn't ate it all at last! Yet every one had had enough, and the youngest Cratchits in particular, were steeped in sage and onion to the eyebrows! But now, the plates being changed by Miss Belinda, Mrs Cratchit left the room alone – too nervous to bear witnesses – to take the pudding up and bring it in.... In half a minute Mrs Cratchit entered – flushed, but smiling proudly – with the pudding like a speckled cannonball, so hard and firm, blazing in half of half-a-quatern of ignited brandy, and bedight with Christmas holly stuck into the top.

Oh, a wonderful pudding! Bob Cratchit said, and calmly too, that he regarded it as the greatest success achieved by Mrs Cratchit since their marriage. Mrs Cratchit said that now the weight was off her mind, she would confess she had had her doubts about the quantity of flour. Everybody had something to say about it, but nobody said or thought it was at all a small pudding for a large family. It would have been flat heresy to do so.

CHARLES DICKENS
A Christmas Carol, 1843

Heap on more wood! – the wind is chill;
But let it whistle as it will,
We'll keep our Christmas merry still.

SIR WALTER SCOTT
Marmion, 1808

Hark! The Herald Angels Sing

Hark! the herald angels sing,
  Glory to the new-born King!
Peace on earth and mercy mild,
  God and sinners reconciled.
Joyful, all ye nations, rise,
  Join the triumph of the skies,
With the angelic host proclaim,
  Christ is born in Bethlehem.

CHARLES WESLEY,
GEORGE WHITEFIELD,
and MARTIN MADEN

Now have good day, now have good day!
I am Christmas, and now I go my way!

ANON

HAPPY NEW YEAR

Sound the Flute

Sound the flute!
Now it's mute.
Birds delight
Day and night;
Nightingale
In the dale
Lark in sky,
Merrily,
Merrily, merrily, to welcome in the Year.

Little boy,
Full of joy;
Little girl,
Sweet and small;
Cock does crow,
So do you;
Merry voice,
Infant noise,
Merrily, merrily, to welcome in the Year.

Little lamb
Here I am;
Come and lick
My white neck;
Let me pull
Your soft wool;
Let me kiss
Your soft face;
Merrily, merrily, we welcome in the Year.

WILLIAM BLAKE

Candlemas Eve

Down with the rosemary, and so
  Down with the bays and mistletoe;
Down with the holly, ivy, all
    Wherewith ye dressed the Christmas hall;
That so the superstitious find
    Not one least branch there left behind;
For look, how many leaves there be
    Neglected there, maids, trust to me,
So many goblins you shall see.

ROBERT HERRICK
Hesperides, 1648

Ring Out Wild Bells

Ring out wild bells to the wild sky,
The flying cloud, the frosty light:
The year is dying in the night;
Ring out, wild bells, and let him die.

Ring out the old, ring in the new,
Ring, happy bells, across the snow:
The year is going, let him go;
Ring out the false, ring in the true.

Ring out the grief that saps the mind,
For those that here we see no more;
Ring out the feud of rich and poor,
Ring in redress to all mankind.

Ring out the want, the care, the sin,
The faithless coldness of the times;
Ring out, ring out my mournful rhymes,
But ring the fuller minstrel in.

Ring out old shapes of foul disease,
Ring out the narrowing lust of gold;
Ring out the thousand wars of old,
Ring in the thousand years of peace.

Ring in the valiant man and free,
The larger heart, the kindlier hand;
Ring out the darkness of the land,
Ring in the Christ that is to be.

ALFRED, LORD TENNYSON
In Memoriam

Good King Wenceslas

Good King Wenceslas looked out
    On the Feast of Stephen,
When the snow lay round about,
    Deep, and crisp, and even:
Brightly shone the moon that night,
    Though the frost was cruel,
When a poor man came in sight,
    Gath'ring winter fuel.

"Hither, page, and stand by me,
    If thou know'st it, telling,
Yonder peasant, who is he?
    Where and what his dwelling?"
"Sire, he lives a good league hence,
    Underneath the mountain,
Right against the forest fence,
    By Saint Agnes' fountain."

"Bring me flesh, and bring me wine,
    Bring me pine logs hither;
Thou and I will see him dine,
    When we bear them thither."
Page and monarch forth they went,
    Forth they went together,
Through the rude wind's wild lament
    And the bitter weather.

"Sire, the night is darker now,
　　And the wind blows stronger;
Fails my heart, I know not how,
　　I can go no longer."
"Mark my footsteps, good my page!
　　Tread thou in them boldly:
Thou shalt find the winter's rage
　　Freeze thy blood less coldly."

In his master's steps he trod,
　　Where the snow lay dinted;
Heat was in the very sod
　　Which the saint had printed.
Therefore, Christian men, be sure,
　　Wealth or rank possessing,
Ye who now will bless the poor,
　　Shall yourselves find blessing.

JOHN MASON NEALE

Robin

Robin sang sweetly
  When the days were bright.
"Thanks! Thanks for Summer!"
  He sang with all his might.

Robin sang sweetly
  In the Autumn days.
"There are fruits for everyone.
  Let all give praise."

In the cold and wintry weather
  Still hear his song.
"Somebody must sing," said Robin,
  "Or Winter will seem long."

When the Spring came back again
  He sang: "I told you so!
Keep on singing through the Winter;
  It will always go!"

ANON

If New Year's Eve Night Wind Blow South

If New Year's eve night wind blow South,
 It betokeneth warmth and growth:
If West, much milk, and fish in the sea;
 If North, much cold, and storms there will be;
If East, the trees will bear much fruit;
 If North-east, flee it man and brute.

TRADITIONAL

The Snowdrops

Where are the snowdrops?" said the sun.
   "Dead!" said the frost,
"Buried and lost
   Every one!"

"A foolish answer," said the sun:
   "They did not die.
Asleep they lie
   Every one!"

"And I will wake them, I, the sun,
   Into the light,
All clad in white
   Every one!"

ANNIE MATHESON

Auld Lang Syne

Should auld acquaintance be forgot,
And never brought to min'?
Should auld acquaintance be forgot,
And auld lang syne?

CHORUS: For auld lang syne, my dear,
For auld lang syne,
We'll take a cup o' kindness yet,
For auld lang syne.

ROBERT BURNS

The Poets and Authors

BURNS, Robert
(1759–1796) UK
Poet and songwriter. Burns, now world-famous as Scotland's greatest minstrel, started his career as a farm-laborer. His verse was first published in 1786 and instantly made him famous. He moved to Edinburgh where, despite a tendency to misbehave, he proved a great success. He married and, with the money earned by his poems and his income as an exciseman, settled down on a small farm at Ellisland. *Auld Lang Syne*, together with *A Red, Red Rose*, *Scots wha hae* and many others, first appeared in James Johnson's *Scots Musical Museum* (1787–1803).

DICKENS, Charles
(1812–1870) UK
The son of a government clerk who was imprisoned for debt, many of the details of Dickens's own childhood of hardship and poverty are mirrored in *David Copperfield*. Dickens had little formal education but became a journalist and, at twenty-four, started to publish the first of his great novels of Victorian life, *The Pickwick Papers*, which appeared in twenty monthly installments. His other works include *Oliver Twist* (1837-8), *A Tale of Two Cities* (1859), and *Great Expectations* (1860-1). With his love of the grotesque, the vitality of his vision and the vividness of his characterization, Dickens created lasting legends of which that of Scrooge in *A Christmas Carol* is surely the most powerful and enduring.

HARDY, Thomas
(1840–1928) UK
Poet and novelist. Initially an architect, Hardy wrote a large number of very popular novels about his native Dorset, including *Tess of the D'Urbervilles (1891)* and *Jude the Obscure (1895)*. He regarded fiction, however, merely as a means of making a living, and longed to write verse. After the publication of *Jude the Obscure*, he gave up novel writing and devoted the rest of his life to poetry. Although they use conventional forms, Hardy's poems are startlingly original in tone and syntax.

HERRICK, Robert
(1591–1674) UK
Poet and parson. The vicar of Dean Prior in Devonshire from 1629 to 1647, Herrick was a charming and witty man who found lyrical poetry easy and natural. His verses range from sensual love poetry to sacred songs, from simple folk ditties to complex imitations of Classical poets. Some twelve hundred of them were published in the *Herperides* (1648).

MOORE, Clement Clarke
(1779–1863) USA
Professor of Biblical Learning in New York, Moore wrote *A Visit from St. Nicholas* for his six children in 1822. The poem was copied into an album, spotted by a family friend and published anonymously in the *Troy Sentinel* the following year. It was immediately popular, but Moore did not reveal himself as the author until 1837.

ROSSETTI, Christina Georgina
(1839–1894) UK
Sister of poet and painter Dante Gabriel Rossetti, Christina led a sad life and failed to fulfill her early exceptional promise. She twice rejected suitors because of her high Anglican religious principles, and her verses are devout and full of the sadness of "what might have been." Her first collection, *Goblin Market* (1862), was very much her finest, but *Sing-Song* (1872) is full of charming, simple verses for children. She was always frail and, at the time of *Sing-Song's* composition, was very close to death from Grave's disease. Thereafter, she taught with her mother and wrote morally improving verse.

SCOTT, Sir Walter
(1771–1832) UK
Novelist and poet. Enormously popular in his own time, Scott's novels such as *Waverly* (1841), *The Antiquary* (1816), *Ivanhoe* (1819), *Kenilworth* (1821), and *Quentin Dunward* (1823), are little read today. Perhaps the most valuable of his works is the *Border Minstrelsy* (1802-3), a collection of traditional ballads of his beloved Scottish Border country. In 1826, James Ballantyne's printing firm, in which Scott was a partner, went bankrupt, ruining Ballantyne and Scott's publisher, Constable. Scott himself was left owing £130,000. Thanks to his unstinting labors, every penny was paid off on Scott's death.

SOUTHEY, Robert
(1774–1843) UK
English Romantic poet, who wrote verse, epic poems and many ballads as well as prose criticism and biography. He married Edith Fricker, whose sister married Coleridge. Southey, in fact, was an associate of Coleridge for some time. In later years his mind gave way and a brief bout of brain fever eventually proved fatal.

STEVENSON, Robert Louis
(1850–1894) UK
A master stylist and supremely imaginative writer who contrived to lead a hero's life despite often crippling illness. All his life he suffered from chronic bronchial problems and acute nervous excitability. Stevenson nonetheless traveled extensively, wrote many fine essays and novels and in *A Child's Garden of Verses* (1885) applied his highly developed gifts of imagination and sympathy to the emotions and enthusiasms of childhood. In so doing he can be said to have invented a whole new genre of verse. In 1888 he travelled in the South Seas and at last settled with his family in Samoa,

where the natives called him "Tusitala" (the tale-teller). He died there of a brain hemorrhage. His novels include *Treasure Island* (1883), *Kidnapped* (1886), *Catriona* (1893), and, for older readers, the eerie *Strange Case of Dr Jekyll and Mr Hyde* (1886).

TENNYSON, Alfred, Lord
(1809–1892) UK
Although the most honored and feted poet of the Victorian era, Tennyson liked to live "far from the madding crowd" in Hampshire or on the Isle of Wight. He was very prolific and, although he never wrote specifically for children, many of his works have become firm favorites with young people because of their grand romantic subject matter or because they are ideal for reciting.

TUSSER, Thomas
(1524–80) UK
Tusser was a homespun poet and philosopher whose *Hundred good pointes of husbandrie* (1557) contained curious, frequently awkward verses giving advice on gardening, farming and house-keeping as well as maxims on good behaviour and good manners.

WESLEY, Charles
(1707–1788) UK
English Methodist clergyman and hymn writer and brother of more famous John Wesley. Charles composed some 6500 hymns and left a journal, which was published in 1849.

WORDSWORTH, William
(1770–1850) UK
Poet Laureate. He lived in Grasmere in the English Lake District with his sister Dorothy. At his best, as in "The Prelude" or "Tintern Abbey," Wordsworth was a brilliant, thoughtful nature poet; at his worst he was capable of gaucheness and banality.

The Painters

A brief note on some of the obscure and unknown poets

Christmas carols and songs have been sung since the very earliest days of Christianity and inevitably, many of the authors are unknown. Because too, Chrismas verse is essentially a popular form, much of this collection has been gleaned from ancient periodicals, news-sheets, and anthologies. Here, though we may find an author's name, there is no biographical information to identify the contributor. I have supplied biographies of the famous poets, but it is often the obscure or unknown poets who have written the most affecting and accessible Christmas verse.

Index of First Lines